Introduction to Revised Edition:

Apart from collecting picture postcards of Folkestone, I have always been interested in photographs from the Victorian era. Asked to prepare this revised edition of *Folkestone – A Photographic Record*, I decided to include some which had not been published before. This revision has resulted in some alteration to the layout of a number of the original pages.

I have included a photograph of the old Kings Arms inn just prior to demolition; how sad its appearance is with bill posters covering the walls. Its successor, the Queens Hotel, is still spoken of today by many local people. One of my first recollections of 1963 – the year I came to Folkestone – is of seeing what had obviously been a fine Victorian building in the hands of the demolition team. Many others followed suit over the years including the Lyndhurst, Esplanade, Majestic and Prince's, all buildings I remember well.

The 1930's saw the demolition of most of the Stade area in a slum clearance scheme. The Beach Street area which had been devastated during the 2nd World War was finally swept away in the 1950's, as was most of the Dover Street area. As a result of this combination of events, Folkestone lost the sort of old fishing quarter which so attracts tourists to Devon and Cornwall. Arriving in 1963 I never saw these old streets, but I did see the last and probably the oldest remaining building of this 'old town' – the Ark Café, which disappeared in contentious circumstances. History will determine the true facts of its passing.

Through my collection of postcards and photographs, and from my conversations with numerous Folkestonians I have come to know and love that part of the town which I never saw as much as the present day Folkestone.

Eamonn D. Rooney
Folkestone, February 1992

I am dedicating this edition to Daphne Heaver, known to all at Copperfields as 'Lady H'. Daphne has constantly impressed me with her love of Folkestone. One ancestor, a gentleman by the name of Crook, is said to have driven one of the first steam engines across the Viaduct and another, Mr. Henry Mercer, was a well known local builder in the 19th century who built Dover Road School and a lot more.

Copyright this edition: John Rice and Eamonn D. Rooney 1992
Published by Alan Sutton Publishing, Phoenix Mill,
Far Thrupp, Stroud, Gloucestershire.
ISBN 0 7509 0262 0
Printed in Great Britain by The Bath Press, Avon.

Thanks are extended to the following for their marvellous co-operation in the research and production of this book:

Roy Green Photographers, Guildhall Camera Centre, Fullers Photography, Lambert Weston Ltd., Halkesworth Wheeler Studios, Folkestone Library and Archives, Folkestone & District Water Company, P.J. Attwater & Co., John Lukey & Sons, Cheriton Furnishers, Oclee Jewellers, Cheriton Post Office, All Souls Church, Cheriton, Rev. Peter Cole, Folkestone Parish Church, Jeremy Miles, Folkestone Herald, George Hazell, New Metropole Hotel, Charles Hamilton, Sky Photos Ltd., Infantry Junior Leaders Battalion, Imperial War Museum, The White Lion, The Lifeboat, The Earl Grey, Ian Standen, Miss Irene Hennings, Mrs. Grace Burke, Mrs. Evelyn Wild and Mrs. Dorothy Humphries.

The 1800's

The lower photograph was taken by Herbert Freeman Brown, an optician in business in George Lane. Since the photograph above was taken, a doorway has been inserted at the corner. Demolition commenced on June 20th, 1882 of both the Kings Arms and the adjoining Liver Stables of Michael Pierrepont Valyer. The opportunity was taken to widen Guildhall Street.

Two early photographs of the Viaduct. This 19-arch, brick-built viaduct was erected under the supervision of William Cubitt, Chief Engineer of the South Eastern Railway Company. Note that at this time (c1857) there was no parapet; this is said to have been added in 1866.

rare photo of the Leas during its early
velopment. This picture was taken about
870.

One of the many serious landslips in the Warren during the past century. This one occurred on January 12th, 1877 when a hug[e] chalk fall blocked the line for two months.

Workers on the proposed Channel Tunnel around 1881.

This view looking out over the harbour from the Leas was probably taken in the 1880's. In the middle distance are the Coastguard Cottages and a terrace of houses fronting the Lower Sandgate Road, all now demolished. An early jetty is visible at the rear of the Harbour Station.

aken in 1886, this was the interior of what
ter became known as the Pleasure Gardens
heatre. Support for the huge exhibition
ntre was not forthcoming so the hall was
nverted to a theatre. Eventually it too
osed in 1960 and nowadays the Orion
surance building occupies the site; in fact
is one of the most beautiful modern
uildings in the entire area as it has retained
sense of lightness and openness and the
loured lights at night make it very
pressive.

Folkestone Harbour in the early 1890's. A number of paddle steamers are moored at the 'Hawk' and the 'Gridiron', two jetties belonging to the South Eastern Railway Company. The buildings in the foreground are the railway company workshops.

The Inner Harbour in 1892. Notice the scaffolding on that beautiful towered house on the hilltop.

Compare this with the photograph above. The towered house – known as Shangri-La – has been completed. In this view, taken in 1894, a pleasure boat is being rowed out of the harbour.

This view of the Leas should be compared with the one below. The photograph may have been taken in the late 1840's or early 1850's, although there is not known to have been a photographer active in Folkestone earlier than 1856. Note how the grass and the cliff edge are not fenced off as in the photograph below. There does, however, seem to be some fencing at the top of what is now the Road of Remembrance.

A view of Albion Villas from the Leas. Notice the old bath chairs, the child in his perambulator on the extreme left and the horse chomping in his nose-bag as his driver chats with an old friend.

Easter 1893 on the Leas. A quiet day – only a couple of carts can be seen outside the Clifton Hotel (on the left). On the right is the statue of William Harvey erected in 1881. The wrought iron railing was added in 1882, but has since been removed.

The Leas Shelter was opened in 1894 as a result of the efforts of the Folkestone Amusements Association. Later, in 1927, it was replaced by the Leas Cliff Hall.

The launching of Folkestone's first lifeboat, the 'J. McConnell Hussey', in 1894. The Lifeboat Station closed down in October 1930 as launches after the 1st World War became fewer and fewer.

A dramatic photo of the wreck of the 'Baron Holberg' which was driven on to the beach between Folkestone's two piers on 25th September, 1896. A hurricane wrecked this ship and also the 'Agdar', both of which were en route for Dublin from the Baltic with cargoes of timber. Crew members from both vessels were rescued either by lifeline or by the Folkestone Lifeboat.

There are not many photographs showing this part of the Leas in the Victorian era. This dates from c1895. Looking towards Clifton Crescent, what is now the Salisbury Hotel is on the right. A group of people rest on one of the many seats provided on the Leas.

Clifton Crescent in the 1890's. The architect purposely left a gap in the crescent so that Holy Trinity Church could be glimpsed from the Leas. Many attempts have been made to gain permission to fill the gap. The crescent suffered enough aesthetic damage when an unsympathetic block of flats was built at the western end.

The men who built the Hotel Metropole
take time off for a group photo, 1896.

Hotel Metropole Folkestone. W.3297.

This photograph shows the Metropole Hotel completed. The late 1890's saw a profusion of these Dutch gables – a leisurely stroll around the West End today will reveal many architectural delights from this period. Note Holy Trinity Church visible on the right.

People promenade on the Leas near the Metropole and Grand Hotels. Note the field on the left, at that time fenced off but today opened up to form part of the Leas.

The 1900's

Though the history of buses in Folkestone is confused, the accepted date of the first service in the town is 1901. This photo is the earliest available of Folkestone Motors Ltd., and it shows Peter Shrubsole, the first man to drive a public service vehicle in Folkestone. The photo was taken either very late in 1902 or early in the new year of 1903. Notice the plaque on the side of the bus advertising a ride from Folkestone to Cheriton for 3d.

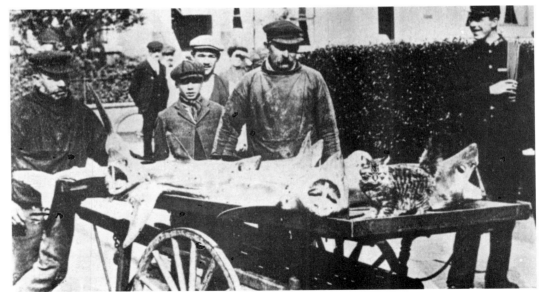

The date is 1910 and these two enterprising fishermen have caught some young sharks off Folkestone. They took their barrow round the town and charged a penny to view the rarely-seen spectacle. Notice the cat on the barrow and the cheerful postman.

The lift, Folkestone.

The Leas Lift just after the turn of the century. The lift was constructed in two stages – the left hand portion in 1885 and the right side in 1890. The extreme right hand part of this building houses the engine which pumps the water back to tanks located under the Leas. The Lift underwent considerable renovation in 1985 on the occasion of its centenary.

FOLKESTONE. — The Cliff Lift. — LL

Such was the popularity of the Leas Lift and the Sandgate Hill Lift that it was decided to construct another nearly opposite the Metropole Hotel. Opened on 31st March, 1904 and called the West Lift, it was popularly known as the Metropole Lift. This lift closed during the 2nd World War.

The Sandgate Hill Lift, which opened on 20th February, 1893, was somewhat different from the others in that the brakeman rode with the car, as was the case at Lynmouth in Devon on which this lift was modelled. However, it was not very successful and finally closed in 1918. The company was wound up on 29th June, 1924.

A busy beach scene. A number of bathing wagons can be seen in the background and a number of rowing boats are pulled up on the foreshore. In the centre of the picture is one of Fagg's Patented Bathing Wagons which were unique to Folkestone. The rail on which this travelled down to the water's edge can clearly be seen.

The Longford Hotel (now the Hotel de France) takes its name from Longford Castle near Salisbury, Wiltshire, home of the Radnor family. The select nature of the Leas is obvious from the 1891 Census – staying here was one John Savill, aged 73, a Peer of the Realm, along with his Valet and one Frederick Holman, Black Rod Officer at the House of Lords.

A very clear photograph of the Marine Gardens shelter in its heyday. The small boy is very interested in the machine just by the path. The top of the bandstand can be seen above the shelter.

A detail of part of the above photograph shows something of the social order of the day. The lady and gentleman walk along whilst the maid brings up the rear carrying the picnic hamper.

Coal Vessel Entering Harbour thro Swing Bridge, Folkestone. H.Bs.Fol. No 203.

The Swing Bridge is open to allow a sailing ship access to the Inner Harbour. The vessel is the 'Cumberland Lassie', a brigantine built at Anglesea in 1874 and registered at Folkestone in 1890. The vessel was owned by John Nelson, an Army Contractor. She was lost at sea in 1918.

A number of sailing ships are moored in the Inner Harbour. The one nearest the camera is the 'Cypress', a brigantine built at Sunderland in 1860 and registered at Folkestone in 1888. The vessel was owned by Richard Godden Saunders. She was sold to the French in 1909.

A crowded scene on the Leas near the Leas Bandstand. A number of bath chairs can be seen and in the centre of the picture is a delightful perambulator. On the right a lady shades herself with a very elegant parasol.

An unusual view looking out over Beach Street and Harbour Street towards the East Cliff. On the extreme right is the Alexandra Hotel, built in 1866 and named after the wife of the first owner, Charles Spurrier.

Many photographs of the Stade have been published over the years but this was too interesting to exclude. Apart from the fishermen and boys on the left, this gives an unobstructed view of the tracks stretching into the distance towards the railway company's workshops. Part of these tracks can be seen to this day.

The Fish Market, Folkestone.

7084

An atmospheric view of one of the fishmarket sheds c1908. Not a lot of work seems to be in hand. Men and boys are standing around; some are showing great interest in the camera. A group of men is standing in the background; perhaps the fishing fleet is due in.

Cheriton's Electric Cinema opened in August 1911 and subsequently featured vaudeville, films, boxing and wrestling. When this photo was taken a film called 'Retribution' was showing and 'Chick's Parade' (some Easter revue perhaps?) was being presented. The site is now a garage though the rear of the building still stands.

Serious damage caused by the Warren landslip on 19th December, 1915.

Local dignitaries entertain the Belgian Consul by taking him for an outing to Canterbury Cathedral in 1915. The location is Sandgate Road and the site was later occupied by Bobby's store in 1934.

This is a very rich photograph of King George V riding through Cheriton in September, 1915. One can almost hear the clip-clop of the horses and the townsfolks' cheers. King George salutes as he passes and to his left, on the white horse, rides Lord Kitchener.

Charlie Banks' circus toured the streets of Folkestone around 1917 entertaining the townspeople and at the same time raising funds for the Victoria Hospital. This photo was taken at the corner of Cheriton Road and Shellons Street.

Originally shot in several sections, this remarkable panoramic view was taken in 1898 and shows Thompson's Patent Gravity Switchback, the Victorian Pier, the Lifeboat Station and bathing cabins.

A wonderful photograph of St Andrew's Convalescent Home. A group of children have spotted the photographer and pose by the fence. The home was founded in Guildhall Street in the 1840's and moved here in the 1890's.

Folkestone Harbour in 1904. The paddle steamer 'Duchess of York' is departing and a train is working up a head of steam as it prepares to leave. In the distance is the Foord viaduct over which another train is steaming.

53474.

A busy scene at the Harbour Pier c1912. Passengers are embarking from the ferry as a large number of people watch from the Harbour Pier. The small crane on the quay is unloading luggage from the wagon parked alongside the passenger train.

...very unusual view on the Stade, possibly in ... late 1890's. The houses in the ...ckground are part of old East Street. This ...s at the far end of the Stade near the East ...ad. The site of the cottages on the right is ...w a series of arches with storage sheds ...der and houses over.

...very crowded beach west of the Victoria ...er between 1901 and 1909. The foreshore ...congested with bathing tents as young and ...d enjoy a day at the seaside.

On the Victoria Pier just after 1900. A
number of people stroll on the pier but
there are not many on the beach. The smal
white building on the beach far right of the
pier is a camera obscura, a Victorian beac
novelty in which the moving scene outside
could be viewed on a screen inside.

It is rarely one sees any views of Augusta
Gardens dating from Victorian and
Edwardian times. This dates from before the
1st World War. It is interesting to note the
lawn laid out for tennis. The house on the
extreme left is thought to be the one in whic
Samuel Plimsoll lived out his last years.

gust 1914 and these German Reservists
re about to embark for the Fatherland but
re arrested and marched up the slope
ow the Road of Remembrance).

n 25th May, 1917 a score of German Gotha
mbers returning from London attacked
lkestone and killed 71 people. It had been
e biggest raid of the war up to that point as
ost raids had been made by Zeppelins or a
w aircraft. Here is the bombed area of
ntine Street.

Mrs Tindall. E. Millen. Mrs H. Holly. H. Croucher. Mrs M Philpott. T Farley. Miss E Jarvis.

S. Winfield. Capt.

F. Orris. R. Leppard. E. Orris.

Ringers on Armistice Day, November 11th, 1918.
Parish Church, Folkestone.

Canon R. J. Tindall. Vicar.

The reticent smiles of these people were a result of camera shyness more than anything else. Inwardly their joy must have been great as this photo was taken at Folkestone Parish Church on November 18th, 1918 – Armistice Day.

is site is now occupied by Cheriton
rnishers but in those days you could buy
most anything at Maycock's store: he
vertised stationery, fancy goods, tobacco
d newspapers – you could even get your
ir shampooed, cut and singed! Compare
day's prices with those on the billboards
ove the shop. 10 Wills cigarettes were 3d,
estward Ho smoking mixture was only 4½d
r ounce and you could relax in the evening
th a Rajah cigar for only 2d! A poster
side the window tells us that 'Black
auty' was showing at the Palace. The
oto was taken in 1922.

On Saturday 19th July, 1919 a Peace Parade took place in Folkestone to celebrate the signing of the peace treaty which officially ended the 2nd World War. The parade commenced at 11a.m., led by the band of the 8th Hussars. This photograph shows British Red Cross nurses lining part of the route.

Crowds throng the pavement and use every vantage point to watch the parade in which nurses, farm girls, WRAFs, WAACs, Folkestone Fisherboys Band and Folkestone Lifeboat took part. The participants pass the saluting point outside the Town Hall.

is photograph shows a section of the
wd dispersing following the Peace
rade of July 1919. The premises on the
, which were then called the Victory Café,
 now the offices of Lunn Poly, a travel
ency.

is was Miss Bridget Kier's Dancing Class
t after the 1st World War. Miss Kier, 'a
dy of Means', did much work for charity
d was very interested in the welfare of
al children. I believe she also painted and
hibited in London frequently.

This photograph was taken in Beach Street, looking towards the railway arches. The date is uncertain but is probably during the flood of 1909. 'Cozzie's' fish and chip shop is fondly remembered by many an old Folkestonian.

A very interesting scene on the foreshore just before the turn of the century. The Port Master's offices and the Harbour Station are visible in the background as are the Marine Gardens and bandstand. The little building on the right is surrounded by people.

The seafront around 1928. Co-operabanc's Coaches would take you to Margate for 5/- and you could have an ice-cream for the journey for 2d.

Radnor Park was laid out in 1886 on a parcel of land given to the town by Lord Radnor. The total cost, including diverting Cheriton Road, was exactly £5,000. The cost of erecting the Lodge alone amounted to £535 15/- 5d.

A view from the tower of the Parish Church in the 1920's. Battery House can be seen among the trees to the left, behind the terrace of houses next to the Bayle Pond. The Harbour, Fishmarket and East Cliff can be seen in great detail.

Foord Road in the 1920's. The omnibus is bound for Hythe, the destination board slung below the windscreen.

A band concert on the Leas around 1930. The huge banners on the pier advertised boating, lunches, picture shows and band music.

A real period piece this photograph, taken on the East Cliff sands in the 1920's. Note the costumes and the parasols – no self-respecting young lady would dream of getting sunburnt in those days – and the pram and push-chair.

East Cliffs and Beach, Folkestone.

Copyright A.F.S. Flk. 44.

On the East Cliff sands c1930, before the building of the promenade. The Martello Tower visible in the background is number 3, now opened as a visitor centre with displays on local history and the Warren. Note the donkeys and their keeper on the right.

The Viaduct in 1933.

Folkestone Fishmarket in 1934. The old tram lines are still to be seen; note the Jubilee Inn just left of centre. A year later a major landslip wrecked many of the buildings but they were rebuilt.

Pleasure boats on the beach near the Victoria Pier in the late 1920's or early 1930's. The one nearest the camera is dressed with bunting and seems to be attracting more custom.

Sealing off Folkestone: coastal defences at the harbour and, at the other end of the town, a concrete blockade at the corner of Cheriton High Street and Risborough Lane.

Damage caused by Parachute Mines on 29th May, 1941 at Morehall Avenue. The death toll amounted to 11 people.

The remains of a German Junkers 87 which collided with houses in Shorncliffe Crescent.

A house in Shorncliffe Road devastated by a Flying Bomb in July 1944.

Barbed wire lines the beach at Sandgate Esplanade.

The old Savoy in Rendezvous Street during the early '50s. Originally intended as a theatre, it became a garage, a skating rink, a cinema and then met the fate of many an old picture house and became a Bingo Hall. It is now a rock music venue and has been renamed the Metronome.

The heyday of the cinema, but now the Odeon is a brand new Boots' store and all of the shops and businesses in this photo have either moved or finished trading. The film showing that week was 'Captain Lightfoot' starring Rock Hudson.

*For over 30 years four or five steam engines
pulled the boat train up the 1 in 30 gradient
from the harbour to the main line. Up front a
'triple head' would pull and a fourth, and even
a fifth engine would push. The old steam engines
were replaced in March, 1959.*

It is 1954 and the last few stanchions of the old pier stand waiting to be torn down. All traces of Victoria Pier finally disappeared in November of that year. (Notice the Crazy Golf Course on top of the Leas Cliff Hall.)

The Light within? An unusual photo of Folkestone Parish Church taken in 1973.

An aerial view of Folkestone town centre taken in the summer of 1972. It shows work commencing on the multi-storey car park and the clearance work for the large Bouverie House. The attractive lawn at the bottom left of the photo is now the site of the Town Walk development and Sainsbury's.

It's the 1970's and the old buildings make way for the new. Here is the Wesleyan Church (built 1864) on Grace Hill being demolished in 1976 to make way for a new office block. On the left is Queens House: compare it with the photo of the Kings Arms (the first photo in this book) which once stood here.

Summing up a few centuries in one striking photograph: on the skyline from left to right are the Welfare building, the Parish Church and the latest addition, Europa House. In the middle distance stands the old Royal Pavilion Hotel (now demolished) and in the foreground the Channel laps continually around the edge of Folkestone. Current plans for a Marina which provide for the filling in of the Inner Harbour will completely alter this view.

Acknowledgements
for Revised Edition:

First of all I would like to thank Vic Seymour for being my liaison with the publisher and for his quiet encouragement. There are many whom I would like to thank for their interest, not least among whom is Frank Root, whose constant interest in this venture (and in Memory Lane) is greatly appreciated. Thanks also to Daphne Heaver ('Lady H') for her unstinting support. I must not forget my very tolerant friends, Chris and Adrian ('we go back to 1415') Munnings at Copylink.